EGYPTIAN MYTHOLOGY

Tales of Egyptian Gods, Goddesses, Pharaohs, & the Legacy of Ancient Egypt.

Dale Hansen

©Copyright 2019 by Cascade Publishing

All rights reserved.

It is not legal to reproduce, duplicate, or transmit any part of this document in either electronic means or in printed format. Recording of this publication is strictly prohibited.

CONTENTS

INTRODUCTION 1

Chapter One The Egyptian Creation Myth 3

    The Early Egyptian Deities (Older Gods) 4

        Isis 4

        The Worship of Isis 6

        Family Tree 7

        Associated Symbols 8

        Osiris 9

        Depictions and Imagery 10

        History 11

        The Worship of Osiris 12

        Resurrection and Everlasting Life 13

        Interesting Facts About Osiris 14

    Younger Egyptian Gods and Other Deities 14

Chapter Two Mythical Creatures, Magic, and Rituals 20

    Ancient Egyptian Demons 20

    Mythical Creatures 21

    Magic and Other Mysterious Rituals 23

        The Priest / Priestess (Magician) 24

        Uses of Ancient Egyptian Magic Rituals 25

        Magic for Healing 26

        Ancient Egyptian Symbols and Their Meanings 27

Chapter Three Funerary Rituals in Ancient Egypt 31

    The Process of Mummification: Three Types 33

    Artifacts and Provisions 34

    Funeral Rites 36

Chapter Four Slavery in Ancient Egypt 37

    Types of Enslavement in Ancient Egypt 38

    The Treatment of Slaves 40

Chapter Five Ancient Egyptian Warfare and Famous Battles 41

    Ancient Egyptian Weaponry 41

    Hyksos Invasion 42

    Egypt and the Canaanite 42

    Egypt and the Hittites 43

Chapter Six Volcanic Eruptions and Revolts in Ancient Egypt 45

Chapter Seven The Seven Year Famine 47

Chapter Eight Tales from Ancient Egypt 50

    The Shipwrecked Sailor 50

    The Battle of Horus and Set 55

Conclusion 57

INTRODUCTION

The Ancient Egyptians have long held people's curiosities. From the majestic yet mysterious pyramids, to the powerful pharaohs who ruled the land—there is much to learn and be fascinated with; and none more so than their deities. The Ancient Egyptians worshipped many gods and goddesses. They watched over the land, delivering punishment where it was due and providing the people with their needs. It is also said that the pharaoh, himself, is akin to the gods. Considered to be their representation on Earth—thus making his word the ultimate law.

Much like the Ancient Greeks, the Egyptians also worshipped their gods through various rituals. They also held many different beliefs and superstitions, which often governed the way they lived. In this book, we will learn more about this ancient society's mysticism, their social hierarchies, as well as the different myths that have woven themselves into their daily lives.

We know of the existence of these myths through various tomb paintings, as well as different artefacts and manuscripts which document the practices related to it. The mythology itself is said to have been underlying Egyptian culture from at least 4000 BCE to 30 CE, which follows the death of Cleopatra VII, who was the last of Egypt's Ptolemaic rulers. Through the fragments of history the ancients have left behind, we can begin to put together a picture of what life was like for them, how they saw the world around them—starting from the very creation to what awaits in the afterlife.

Ancient Egypt's religious beliefs were also passed along and influenced many other cultures. It became particularly wide-spread when the Silk Road opened in 130 BCE. At the time, Alexandria was Egypt's main port city which also served as a commercial center where trade materialized. Egyptian Mythology was said to have been instrumental when it came to creating the concept of the afterlife—or an eternal life after one has died. It has also influenced other cultures' concept of reincarnation as well as the existence of deities. In fact, both Plato and Pythagoras were said to have been influenced by Egyptian beliefs, whilst the religious culture of Rome also borrowed plenty from these ancient myths.

The Ancient Egyptians understood human existence as merely a small segment of our eternal journey, one that is set into motion by supernatural forces greater than us. These are the deities which comprise the Egyptian Pantheon. As for their concept of the afterlife, they likened it to a reflection of the life lived at present. It is for this reason that they also believed the present must be lived well in order for an individual to enjoy the rest of the eternal journey.

This is something we'll get to learn more as we continue our own journey into discovering more about Egyptian Mythology.

Shall we begin?

CHAPTER ONE

The Egyptian Creation Myth

The Egyptians believed that man's eternal journey began at the very creation of the world, and the universe. Their belief is that once, there was nothing more than endless dark water; one without any purpose of form. However, within this void existed Heka, the god of magic, who quietly awaited the point of creation. From this dark water rose Ben-Ben, a primordial hill, and upon whose peak stood Atum. The god looked upon the darkness ('Nu'), and saw that he was alone. Through magic, Atum mated with his own shadow and eventually gave birth to two divine children. These were Shu, the god of air; and Tefnut, the goddess of moisture. It was Shu who gifted this young world with the principles of life, whilst Tefnut provided it with the principles of order.

The two left their father atop Ben-Ben as they began their mission to establish the world. However, Atum grew concerned after some time as his children had been gone for so long. To search for them, he removed his eye and sent it out into creation. While he awaited the return of his children, Atum sat alone and contemplated eternity, in the midst of the chaos around him. Eventually, Shu and Tefnut would return with their father's eye. This all-seeing eye is one of the most recognizable symbols of Ancient Egypt and this is its origin.

With his children safely home, Atum was overcome with joy and began to shed tears of happiness. These tears dropped onto the dark, yet fertile earth of Ben-Ben, which led to the birth of mortal men and women.

The Early Egyptian Deities (Older Gods)

After the birth of mankind, Shu and Tefnut recognized that they had no place to live in. Knowing Ben-Ben will not be enough to sustain them, the two gods mated and gave birth to Nut, who is the representation of the sky; and Geb, who represented the earth. Despite being brother and sister, Geb and Nut fell deeply in love, becoming inseparable. Atum, however, was against their union and so he took Nut away from Geb and placed her high up in the heavens so they would no longer be able to touch.

This was in vain, however, for Nut was already pregnant, and she eventually gave birth to the earliest known gods in Egyptian Mythology: Isis, Osiris, Nephthys, Set, and Horus. They are also the most recognized of the deities.

Isis

Isis is known as the "Goddess with Ten Thousand Names", an exaggeration in number but it does point to the fact that she has been called a multitude of names, and has been given many different titles. To provide you with an idea, Isis is also known as:

- Aset
- Eenohebis
- Aust
- Esu

- Eset
- Iahu
- Hesat
- Urethekau
- Unt
- Werethekau

Some of her known titles include:

- The Queen of All Gods
- The Divine One
- The Maker of Sunrise
- Queen of Heaven
- Mother of God

Isis was also closely associated with other Egyptian goddesses such as Hathor and Sekhmet. She was also worshipped by the Greeks, and related her to their own goddesses; Tethys, Athena, and Persephone.

As a deity, she also held many different roles. The most important of which are:

- She was the wife of Osiris, and is also the mother of Horus.
- Isis was also known as a fertility goddess. This is among the many reasons why many women worshipped her.
- She was also known as a goddess of magic and many people would turn to her, and her cult for different spells to help them solve their problems. According to certain myths, Isis was able to trick Ra into telling her his secret name; and in doing so, the goddess was able to obtain numerous magical powers.

With the different roles she fulfilled in the Egyptian Pantheon, Isis was also given a name associated with:

- Usert – Goddess of the earth
- Khut – Giver of light at every new year
- Satis – The flood power of the Nile
- Thenenet – Goddess of Tuat, also known as the Underworld
- Kekhet – Goddess of cultivated areas and the fields
- Ankhet – Provider of fertility from the waters, and the embracer of the land
- Tcheft – Goddess of the good offered by humans to the gods
- Renenet – Goddess of the Harvest
- Ament – Lady of the Underworld; she is said to restore the bodies of the dead so that they may live with Osiris in his kingdom.

The Worship of Isis

Isis had cults which were spread, not only throughout Egypt, but also in different fragments of Europe. People worshipped the goddess as the ideal, fertile mother. Women, in particular, comprised as her primary worshippers. She was also honored through images and statues which were preserved in her temples. Isis was also part of a triad of powerful deities which included Osiris and Horus.

In imageries, she was often depicted as nursing Horus or the pharaoh. It is said that certain aspects of her role as a mother could have also influenced the earliest Christian concepts about the Virgin Mary. The priests who worshipped Isis were believed to have been able to cure illness, and they often celebrated different festivals which were dedicated to her alongside her four siblings. These festivities would often take place on five successive days during the end of the year.

There are two primary temples located in Egypt which are known to have been dedicated to the goddess. These temples include Philae and Behbeit el-Hagar. Behbeit el-Hagar's construction began around the Late Period and was most commonly used during the Ptolemaic Period. The temple was built by the kings of the Ancient Kingdom's Thirtieth Dynasty who followed Isis with fervent devotion. Behbeit el-Hagar was also a match to the temple at Philae, located in Upper Egypt.

The temple located in the island of Philae was constructed much earlier, around the Twenty-fifth Dynasty. However, it did not become a prominent temple up until the Greco-Roman period. In the 1960's, this temple was actually moved by scholars in order to save it from submerging underwater following the construction of the Aswan Dam.

Family Tree

- Father: Geb, the god of the earth
- Mother: Nut, the goddess of the sky
- Brother and Husband: Osiris, the god of the dead and of resurrection
- Brother: Set, the god of evil and darkness
- Sister: Nepthys, the goddess of darkness, decay and death
- Son: Horus, a sky god. Also known as the god of kingship.
- Son: Anubis, the god of embalming. In mythology, Anubis was actually the son of Nepthys by either Set or Osiris. However, he was abandoned by his mother as an infant and was found by Isis, who later raised him as her own.
- Son: Mesthi, guardian of the deceased's liver contained in a Canopic jar. He was also guardian of the South.
- Son: Hapi, guardian of the deceased's lungs contained in a Canopic jar. He was also guardian of the North.

- Son: Qep-Sennuf, guardian of the deceased's intestines contained in a Canopic jar. He was also the guardian of the West.
- Son: Tuamutef, guardian of the deceased's stomacn contained in a Canopic jar. He was also guardian of the East.

Associated Symbols

Like the other Egyptian gods, there are also a few symbols that are deeply associated with the goddess. The first would be the SEPT, which is a star that marks the beginning of a brand new year, as well as the beginning of the Nile's flooding. Next, we have the THET which is the knot or buckle of Isis. The Thet is also thought to represent a uterus, though stylized. It was also usually made of a red substance, and symbolized blood and life.

Isis also associated with sacred animals including a snake, cow, and a scorpion. Her sacred birds were a vulture, hawk, and dove.

In the many depictions of the goddess, she was often shown as a human woman. She wore a vulture headdress, with its head extended like a crown over her forehead whilst its wings hung down each side of her head. Isis was also shown wearing a bejeweled collar and a floor-skimming gown. In these images, she often held a scepter and a papyrus, as well as an ankh in her hands. She was also typically portrayed donning long wings.

In certain images, however, the headdress is replaced with a crown. These crowns tend to vary in style, with some bearing horns surrounding a sun disc. In others, the horns are that of a ram which is intended to associate her with Osiris. The goddess was not always dressed in full regalia—in the depictions where she is shown to be a mortal woman, she wears simpler clothing, though her headdress contains a uraeus symbol.

Osiris

Osiris in Egyptian Mythology existed as the god of the underworld. He is also one of the earliest gods and has quite a history associated to his name. To be more specific, Osiris was god of the dead, of the afterlife, and the underworld. In different depictions, he was often shown as a man who had green skin with a beard that's also connected with the pharaohs. Osiris also wore a crown that bore two large ostrich feathers and his legs were partially wrapped with cloth, in the same manner as a mummy. In his hands, he held a flail and a symbolic crook.

Much like Isis, he too had a number of different names. It must be noted, however, that Osiris is actually a Latin word. The original Egyptian hieroglyphs rendered his name as Wsjr. There are also Egyptologists who refer to him as:

- Ausar
- Aser
- Asari
- Asar
- Usire
- Ausare
- Wser
- Usir
- Wesir

Translated in English, his name means "Almighty" or "The Powerful One". This was how the Ancients perceived the deity, certainly worshipped with prayer and rituals for thousands of years. Osiris, as the Ancient Egyptians believed, was among the most powerful of the gods. But, aside from being the god of the underworld, he was also worshipped as the shepherd god.

Evidence of which can be seen in the shepherd's crook which he was often depicted with.

Osiris has many titles, too. His name first appeared during the Fifth Dynasty of the kingdom, however, it has been said that he was already being worshipped since the First Dynasty. There are also mentions of him in much later Egyptian documents, particularly in the Contending of Horus and Seth, the various writings of Ancient Greek authors, and on the Shabaka Stone.

Among his titles are, the "King of the Living" and "Foremost of the Westerners". These were given to Osiris because of his role as ruler of the underworld and of the dead, whom the Ancients referred to as The Living Ones of the Westerners. As a deity, he was considered to be a merciful judge of those entering the afterlife. He is also credited for the fertile flooding of the river Nile, which allowed for vegetation to flourish thus granting everyone a means of life. His other titles include: The Lord of Silence, He Who Is Permanently Benign and Youthful, and the Lord of Love.

Depictions and Imagery

In the many ancient paintings of Osiris, he was given green or black skin. The green was believed to be a color that the Ancient Egyptians associated with rebirth. Black, on the other hand, was a color that's associated with fertility. This was the color of fertile soil that stretched across the plains every year, each time that the Nile overflowed. This annual event played a significant role in Egypt's prosperity.

There are also some instances wherein Osiris was shown to be wearing a crown that featured a rendering of the moon. Some Egyptologists and researches think that he might have also been associated with either the night or the moon.

History

As we have established earlier, Osiris is one of the five children born to the goddess of the sky and the god of the earth. Through this family line, he is also a great-grandson of the Egyptian god, Ra. Osiris' story is deeply interwoven with that of his four younger siblings, the same deities who will play significant roles in his story.

As the first born son, it was Osiris who was meant to inherit the throne of Egypt. Seth married Nephthys and Osiris married Isis. Together, the two of them became quite powerful—but their marriage was not destined for happiness. A theme that appeared to be common in the lives of different deities, and the Egyptian Pantheon remained no exception.

We begin with Nephthys who magically transformed herself and took on the appearance of Isis, seducing Osiris and presenting herself to him as his wife. Completely oblivious to the trickery, Nephthys became pregnant by Osiris and gave birth to their son, Anubis.

His brother Seth also developed a vendetta against him; this is said to be because of the fact that Osiris inherited the throne to Egypt or because of the fact that he had also gotten Seth's wife pregnant. Whilst the reason remains unclear, Seth did plot to kill his brother. First, he lured Osiris into a coffin and drowned him in the Nile. The annual flooding of the great river is said to represent this event in the deity's life.

After this incident, Isis did manage to recover Osiris' body, but Seth remained stealthy and managed to steal Osiris' lifeless body not too long after. He cut up his brother's figure and hid the remnants across the Egyptian desert. But the connection between Isis and Osiris was unbreakable, and so strong, that the goddess expended years upon years searching for each mutilated part of her husband's body. Eventually, Isis was successful in managing to find all of the fragments, except for one, and it was believed that she cast her powers to construct Osiris back together again.

There are endless numbers of different versions to how this particular story ends, but after restoring her husband's body, it is understood that Isis became pregnant giving birth to a son, Horus. Ultimately, Osiris later died, and descended to the underworld where he assumed his duty as ruler.

Now, there are also other stories which suggest how Osiris took over several underworld duties from his son, Anubis. In other versions, it is believed that the roles were his right given the fact that he was the first god to have died. Among his chief roles was to judge the souls of the dead.

The Worship of Osiris

In Ancient Egypt, the people included the worship of Osiris as an important part of their daily life. The story of his murder by Seth and his 72 accomplices is retold annually, as part of this worship. They saw it as a story of rebirth and regeneration, one which played out every year with the cyclical flooding of the Nile River. The land of Egypt was fertile and is one of the breadbaskets of the Ancient World. This is something that the ancients attributed to Osiris and as such, they would have many ceremonies to show their gratitude. The people would praise his name, his attributes, and his actions.

Recognized as the first king of Egypt, the symbols that were associated with Osiris, the shepherd's staff and the flail, also became essential symbols to the pharaohs who continued his reign. His legacy was seen as the ideal, one which many succeeding kings attempted to emulate. To his people, Osiris represented a time of fertility, unity, and peace.

He was the good shepherd who was beloved by the people. Venerating him was seen as a means of keeping Egypt and her people prosperous. The worship of Osiris was also believed to ensure fertility and plentiful crops along the banks of the river Nile.

Resurrection and Everlasting Life

It is believed that the dead rulers of Egypt would rise along with Osiris, and inherit eternal life. However, a new version of this became widespread during Egypt's New Kingdom. The new belief was that it wasn't just the old, dead kings who would rise along with the god, but also any Egyptian who performed the necessary rituals as well. It is this belief that associated Osiris with new life and death, also why he was commonly correlated with the different cycles of nature.

The worship of Osiris continued on, even while Christianity was on the rise. This was a time when the Romans began suppressing the Ancient Egyptian religion and was actively promoting Christianity to the land's people. Though faced by this, the Egyptians continued to worship, revere, and even made sacrifices to Osiris secretly.

Resurrection is another theme that's commonly associated with Osiris. His slaying at the hands of his brother represented, for the Ancient Egyptians, a new beginning after good has defeated evil. They saw it as a representation of the sun disappearing into the underworld each night, only to be reborn the following day.

Now, for some people, the story of Osiris might seem quite familiar. In many ways, the elements of his story is also similar to the death and resurrection of Jesus Christ. However, their stories differ when it comes to what ensues in the afterlife.

For the Ancient Egyptians, they believed that deities such as Osiris, Anubis, Ammut, Henefer, Ma'at, and Thot would welcome a person's soul once they reach the afterlife. Upon arrival, these deities would perform the "weighing of the heart" ceremony. Basically, the individuals heart would be weighed against Ma'at's feather. If the heart was lighter, it symbolized that they lived an honest, respectable life and would subsequently be allowed to enter the kingdom of Osiris where they would occupy the rest of eternity.

Interesting Facts About Osiris

- Osiris ranks as one of Egypt's most important deities.
- Whilst his origins remain quite obscure, Osiris was known to have been a local deity in Busiris, which is a city in Lower Egypt.
- Osiris held a temple in Abydos and this is where he was primarily worshipped.
- Later, he was also worshipped as a Hellenistic god and was given the name Serapis.
- Many Greco-Roman writers associated him with the Greek God, Dionysus.
- Recently, archaeologists were able to unearth a 3,200 year old replica of Osiris' tomb. This was located in Sheikh Abd el-Qurna on the West bank of the Thebes.

Younger Egyptian Gods and Other Deities

The Ancient Egyptian Religion was quite polytheistic, which means that they worshipped many different gods and goddesses. In fact, if we were to count them all, there are about 2000 known Egyptian deities.

Quite a lot, huh?

These gods and goddesses played significant roles when it came to the daily lives of the Ancient Egyptians. They were also divided into two levels: The Local Gods and The National Gods. The people looked to these deities for help with just about everything; from helping them beat children, to growing their crops, and their safe journey into the afterlife. There were also daily rituals meant to care for the gods, and festivals which celebrated specific deities.

Some of the most important deities in the Egyptian Pantheon include:

Amun – He was a creator god whose rank rose to national deity following the moving of the capital to the city of Thebes. Later, he was combined with Ra. The people believed that *Amun-Ra* was the creative force behind all that exists in life. He was known to be the god of the pharaohs, and represented fertility, the wind, and secrets.

Ra – He was a sun-god, a creator god, and also the king of the gods. He is considered to be the father of the deities and is typically depicted as having the body of a human, but with the head of a falcon.

Hathor – She was a cow goddess, as well as a cosmic goddess. She is said to have nourished all life on earth with her milk. Her name means "House of Horus". In certain legends, she is given the role of Horus' consort and together with their son Ihi, they formed a triad of deities.

Horus – He was a sun god and also the king of the gods. The title "The Living Horus" was given to the pharaoh as a means of emphasizing his right when it comes to ruling Egypt. Basically mirroring how Ra ruled the gods. His emblem was the falcon, and he is also known as being one of the Osirian gods. The others include Osiris, Isis, Set, and Nephthys. One of the most recognizable symbols that's associated with Egypt is the Eye of Horus, and this symbolized great power.

Isis – She was a fertility goddess, who is also known as a mother deity. She was Osiris' sister-wife, and the mother of the god Horus. Among the many legends surrounding her, one of the most famous would be her effort to restore the body of her husband after he was assassinated. This stands out because it was also at this point when she impregnated herself with his restored body, conceiving Horus in the process.

Ma'at – She was the divine representation of moral and physical law. Many Egypt scholars also consider her as the most important goddess of Ancient Egypt. She was worshipped throughout the land for she was among those who judged the dead.

Osiris – He was the god of the dead and of resurrection. He was also the ruler of the Tuat and its people would often seek him and appeal that he care for their departed ancestors. Osiris also ruled as king of the gods until he was murdered by his brother.

Set – Also known as Setekh, he was the god of darkness and evil. He was also an adversary of Horus and of everything that was good. With the exception of the red crown, the people of Ancient Egypt thought of the color red as a symbol of evil because of its association with Set. He was also associated with storms, deserts, strength, and war.

Anubis – One of the most recognizable Egyptian deities, he was the god of the dying and of death. He was also considered to be god of the underworld, a role which he would eventually share with Osiris. It is his image that often adorned Ancient Egyptian tombs as the people saw him as a protector and guardian.

Sobek – He was a crocodile god. In his many depictions, he was often shown as being a complete crocodile or a combination between human and crocodile. He symbolized the might and strength of the pharaohs.

Aten – Aten was a sun god who was worshipped by the Pharaoh Akhenaten. His origin, as a deity, is mostly unknown. The hymns written for him, at least the ones that survived, show that worshipping him was quite a joyful event. Unlike the other deities, he does not have a humanoid shape. In the depictions we know of him, he is portrayed as a sun disc and his rays that extend from this form had hands on each end. There are images of the royal family which show them worshipping Aten and this can be found at Tell el-Amarna.

Bastet – She was a cat goddess and was also a patroness of pregnant women. Bastet was well known to have loved dance and music, marking the festival at Bubastis one of the most popular in the whole of Egypt. According to different records, these festivities are attended by as many as 700,000 people. She was also seen by the Ancient Egyptians as a representation of the sun's powers. In depictions of her, Baster is sometimes shown as a woman who had a cat's head or simply as a complete cat. People also mummified cats as a way of honoring the goddess.

Geb – He was the personification of the Earh and the father of the five Osirian gods. His symbol was the goose and in some of his known depictions, Geb is shown as a man with a goose upon his head. Other images show him as a man who laid beneath Shu's feet, while Nut was stretched above them. He was said to have had green or black skin, thought to represent the Earth's fertility.

Nut – She was Geb's consort and was also the personification of the sky. She is the mother of the Osirian gods and was represented by the sycamore tree. The Ancient Egyptians believed that she provided the dead with food. According to legend, in order for Nut to give birth to the Osirian gods, Thoth had to win enough moonlight in order to create the five new days needed for her to do so. In depictions of the deity, she is often shown as a woman carrying a jar of water on her head. There are also other images which portray her as a woman veiled with stars all over her body, while she arches across the heavens above Shu and Geb.

Nephthys – She was one of the Osirian gods and personified decay, darkness, and death. She was said to have been a friend to the dead and also helped in reconstructing Osiris' body following his murder at the hands of Set. As a deity, Nephthys also represented reproduction, regeneration, and virility. She was also a goddess of healing; often depicted as a woman wearing the symbol representing her name on her head and adorned with long wings.

Sekhmet – She was a lion goddess who was also the deity of war and battle. Known to be a great hunter or warrior goddess. Quite the opposite of the goddess Bastet, there are legends which claim Sekhmet to be another aspect of Hathor. She was also part of the Memphis Triad together with Nefertem and Ptah. In the many depictions of the goddess, she is shown to be a woman who had a lioness' head and was crowned by a sun disc surrounded by the ureaus.

Ptah – He was known as a craft deity and was also a protector of artists, and artisans. According to myths about him, Ptah made use of his skills as a metal smith in order to create the other gods. He was primarily worshipped in Memphis and was part of the Triad together with Sekhmet and their son, Nefertem. His priests thought of the Apis bull as the living representation of the deity. In his many depictions, he is shown as an older man who wore a tight garment.

Shu – He was the god of air. Among his duties was to keep his children, Geb and Nut, away from each other. His consort was Tefnut and together, they were the first couple of a group of gods called the Heliopolis Ennead. In depictions of him, Shu was often shown as a man who wore feathers atop his head and carried a staff. There are other versions of his imagery which showed him holding the four pillars of heaven between his arms.

Tefnut – She was the goddess of moisture and also the consort of Shu. Alongside him, she was part of the Great Ennead and aided in supporting the sky. In some legends, Tefnut was depicted as a bloodthirsty and furious lioness. In fact, some of her depictions show the deity as a woman with the head of a lioness, likewise to many of the other deities.

Do note that the Egyptian Pantheon consists of thousands of deities and the above list is comprised of the most recognizable ones—it is by no means comprehensive. There are also instances wherein two gods are combined or are associated with each other to the point where they become one in the same.

Chapter Two

Mythical Creatures, Magic, and Rituals

When it comes to Egyptian mythology, it can oftentimes be a little tricky to differentiate monsters and mythical creatures from the deities themselves. As we have established in the previous chapter, many of these gods and goddesses take on animal forms, which can lead to people mistaking them for beasts of legends. In this chapter, we'll get to know some of the most recognizable creatures from Egyptian mythology in order to better understand what differentiates them from the rest.

Ancient Egyptian Demons

Ammit – She was known as the "devourer of the dead" and was both a goddess, as well as a demoness in Ancient Egyptian religion. She was said to have had a body that was part hippopotamus, part lion, and part crocodile. These are three of the biggest "man-eaters" known to the ancients. As a funerary deity, she was also referred to as the "Eater of Hearts". Her job was to devour the hearts of the deceased which were judged to be impure, thus rendering the soul of the person unable to continue their journey to Osiris and immortality. It was also said that after

Ammit devours a heart, the soul of the person whom it belonged to would remain restless for eternity—essentially receiving a second death.

Apep – Also known as Apophis, he was the direct opponent of light and of Ma'at. He is depicted as a giant serpentine creature and his myth often centers on the many battles he has had against the god, Ra. In myths, he changes locations very often—this particular detail gained him the title "World Encircler". He was said to have had a roar so loud and terrifying, it made the underworld rumble. His movements were believed to have caused earthquakes. His battles with Set may have also been meant as a way for the ancients to explain where thunderstorms came from.

Ammit and Apep are just two examples of demons mentioned in Ancient Egyptian religion. They have the most detailed backgrounds in comparison to the others. In certain cases, the god Set is also mentioned in this category—with him being the god of darkness and all that is evil. There are a few others such as Kek and Shezmu, but their backgrounds are a bit vaguer and less detailed compared to Ammit and Apep.

Mythical Creatures

Gryphon – When it comes to the recognizable creatures out of Egyptian Mythology, the Gryphon or the Griffin is among the most infamous. To begin with, there's plenty of modern references to it; whether it be in films and books. Even stories that don't necessarily deal with Egyptian myths have taken inspiration from this creature of lore. It was said to have the body, back legs, and tail of a great lion, the head and the powerful wings of an eagle, and deadly talons for its front feet.

Because the lion and eagle were considered to be the kings of their kind, the Gryphon was seen as an extremely powerful beast. They were best known for guarding priceless possessions and treasures. In classical antiquity, these creatures were often associated with gold. In certain lore, were also thought to have laid eggs deep down in burrows within the ground, and that these nests also contained nuggets of gold. Their claws were believed to have medicinal properties and that the Gryphon's feathers had the power to restore sight to the blind.

Gryphons existed in both Greek and Egyptian myth. However, their imagery was quite widespread as there's also evidence of them existing in Ancient Iranian art, in Syria, and Anatolia during the Middle Bronze Age.

Sphinx – Much like the Gryphon, Sphinxes are not exclusive to Egyptian Mythology. There are many variations of the half-human, half-lion creature which can be found in places such as Greece and Turkey. However, it has become associated with Egypt because of the Great Sphinx that can be found in the desert of Giza. This has become a national symbol for the country as well and is the most recognizable of its landmarks.

As for the myths, there are two distinct differences between the Egyptian sphinx and that of the Greek or Turkish variety. The former is described as being even-tempered and is said to be male. The latter, on the other hand, are often depicted as female and have a comparably more aggressive disposition. In terms of their role, however, they are supposed to zealously guard riches or in some cases, repositories of wisdom, and will not permit any traveler to pass through unless they are capable of solving one of their difficult riddles.

Bennu – According to certain sources, Bennu is the ancient source of what we now know as the phoenix myth. Benny was a bird god, a fire bird to be exact, and was a familiar of Ra. In certain myths, Bennu animated the spirit which fueled world's creation. One story envisions a fire bird that is understood to have flown over the primordial waters known as Nun. Bennu was also often associated with the theme of resurrection and rebirth; he would be later immortalized by Herodotus as the phoenix, describing the creature as a massive red and gold bird. He believed that Bennu was born anew every single day, in the same way the sun rises and sets.

Only later will more details be added to this; such as the bird's "destruction" by fire, only to be reborn from its own ashes.

Serpopard – The name is a portmanteau of "serpent" and "leopard" which is taken from the creature's image; that it had the body of a leopard and the neck and head of serpent. For the Ancient Egyptians, the Serpopard was a symbol of the chaos which ruled the land that's beyond the borders of Egypt—something which the king is tasked to tame. In depictions, Serpopards are often shown as restrained or conquered; they might also be shown attacking other animals. There are variations of the creature in Mesopotamian art where they are shown in pairs with their long necks intertwined.

These are just a few of Egypt's ancient mythological creatures. They are among the most recognizable and whose influence has managed to span beyond the borders of Egypt. In some cases, especially in more recent myths, it's the ancient Egyptians who were influenced by other cultures. Such is the case with El Naddaha, also known as the Nile's siren—she isn't on this list because scholars argue that she's more of djinn and is therefore of Muslim origins.

Magic and Other Mysterious Rituals

For us, magic is often nothing more than an illusion—smoke and mirrors—meant to trick the eye. However, for the Ancient Egyptians, it was part of daily life and was a way for them to communicate with the gods. Through it, they would ask for guidance, for luck, and it also acted as a medium for them to interact with the spiritual world.

The Ancient Egyptians referred to this practice as **Heka** and even today, it remains to be one of the most mysterious practices in the world. These are rituals which usually took place in their grand temples without an audience. So how do we know of its existence? There are plenty of everyday life artifacts from this time which demonstrates that even regular people practiced their own "form" of such magic; and it is their belief that by doing so, they grow closer to the gods and to what their heart desires.

Many of the objects related to the practice of Heka were actually discovered in tombs. As there are a significant number of preserved ancient tombs, scholars have also discovered plenty of fascinating inscriptions which refer to the magical practices used in daily life. The name Heka actually comes from one of the oldest deities in the Egyptian pantheon. He was presented in human form, making people relate to him more when compared to the other deities.

The Priest / Priestess (Magician)

We know of modern magicians as showmen, but back in Ancient Egypt they were actually provided the same education as priests. They would learn the same myths and invoke the same gods and goddesses during their practice. Most of the time, they were the same person and can assume either role depending on the ceremony and its purpose.

These roles also differed depending on who they were serving. For example, whenever they attended to the royal family, particularly the pharaoh, they were referred to as priests. They were given the task of performing critical rituals which were deemed central to the overall preservation of the kingdom. These rituals are part of the so-called "calendar magic" wherein rituals are performed during specific hours of the day, as well as on designated days of the year.

When they operated within the general public, however, they assumed the role of magician. That said, there's little difference when it comes to the rituals they performed. They would call upon the same deities using the same magic, except this is carried out in the temples and in full view of an audience. Needless to say, the magician converts to a priest when in private practice.

Now, these ancient magicians played an important role when it came to orthodox religion. They would use spells as a means of protecting the royal family and knew of the different rituals that would help dispel the forces of darkness. It was well accepted by the people that evil will never be truly conquered, however, as depressing as this might be, it was balanced with their belief that these negative energies can be contained through rituals and ceremonies.

Uses of Ancient Egyptian Magic Rituals

As discussed earlier, the Ancient Egyptians believed that there are evil forces around them that could harm them if they failed to protect themselves accordingly. These threats could come from a number of different sources, including demons, people who practiced dark magic, and even angry gods. Protection from these negative forces is often gained through magic rituals and practices, as well as amulets which they wore to keep evil away.

Protective rituals are also performed during moments in life which renders an individual vulnerable, such as during childbirth. The same is also used to protect a soul's journey into the underworld; and as we all know, the Egyptians had very complex funerary rituals which are all meant to guide and protect the deceased's spirit.

Magic for Healing

As you might imagine, the time of the ancients was also plagued with many health hazards and diseases that claimed the lives of many—both young and old. The environment was often unforgiving; the Nile had parasites and the sand caused respiratory problems for the people. Whilst the Ancient Egyptians had medical practices which were quite advanced for the time, they had no cure for every ailment. It is also important to note that some of these health issues were also sometimes attributed to the gods or harmful curses cast upon the individual. For these cases, the people turned to magic for a cure.

The previously mentioned priests were not only well-versed in protective and healing incantations, they were also medically trained and often called upon for help with medical complications. The most interesting being their method of healing, which combined medical practice with magical rituals. They made use of spells and worship meant for specific gods and goddesses. In particular, the gods Sekhmet and Selqet were often called upon. They were the goddesses of the plague and the scorpion (venom and bites), respectively.

Some of the known techniques the priests used include:

- Acting out a myth with the patient through the recitation of different spells and speeches.
- The use of natural substances such as dung or honey in order to lure out and repel demons that may have possessed the patient.
- Inscribing healing and protective spells on amulets and statues.

- They may also use magic wands as a means of summoning powerful beings or for drawing protective circles.
- Noise was also seen as a way to ward off evil spirits. Priests would often make loud sounds by shouting or stamping their feet. They may also perform ritualistic dances using drums and the sistra.
- There were also special bowls, with spells inscribed upon them, which were believed to turn water into healing potions. This was either drunk or used to wash a patient with.
- Animal blood is also sometimes mixed into the potions on order to strengthen its potency.
- They also had wax figures of people made which were used to curse enemies, similar to voodoo dolls.

Ancient Egyptian Symbols and Their Meanings

Ancient Egypt still remains one of the most mysterious and despite its popularity in pop culture, our understanding of their spirituality, culture, and mythology is quite limited. The things that we do know, we were able to derive from the surviving hieroglyphs—many of which depicted the events which occurred during the age of pharaohs. Their culture was rife in symbolism, many of which have made its way into modern consciousness and has become part of our own as well.

Below are a few examples of Egyptian symbolism and their meaning:

- **Ankh**

The Ankh is, arguably, one of the most recognizable symbols of ancient Egypt. It is also known as crux ansata, a name given to it by Coptic Christians. This symbol represents immortality and life. It has also been used to represent the union between men and women—of Osiris and Isis, in particular, which was believed to be the cause of the Nile's flooding. This is also one of the reasons why the Ankh is referred to as the Key of the Nile. They also believed the Ankh to be a key to eternity or a key to the underworld.

Ankhs were often drawn upon temple walls as they believed it provided them divine protection.

- **The Eye of Horus**

Another popular Egyptian symbol, the Eye of Horus represented healing, protection, health, and royal power. It is also seen as a symbol of the moon and was often used as a medical tool for measuring ingredients whenever the priests prepared medicine.

According to one myth, Set and Horus were fighting about who would replace Osiris after the deity's death. It was during this point that Set gouged Horus' left eye. Hathor cast magic in an attempt to heal his eye and Horus later offered it to his father, in order to bring him back to life. This is also one of the reasons why the Eye of Horus is seen as a symbol of sacrifice.

The "all-seeing eye", also referred to as the Eye of Providence, that's often seen as a Masonic symbol was also derived from this.

- **The Eye of Ra**

There are many different legends behind the origin of this symbol. However, a lot of scholars agree that the Eye of Ra was actually Horus' right eye. The two symbols represented very similar concepts. There are also myths that talk of the symbol being a personification of many different goddesses, including: Hathor, Wadjet, Bastet, Sekhmet and Mut.

Ra is the god of the sun in Egyptian mythology, this makes the symbol representative of the sun as well.

- **Ouroboros**

In Egyptian mythology, the Ouroboros was one of the symbols of the sun and it was representative of Aten's travels. It also represented the recreation of life, rebirth, and perpetuity. In the Book of the Dead, the symbolism of a snake eating its tail / snake consuming itself, was also associated with Atum. According to the myth, he was born from the waters of Nun and took on the form of a serpent which renewed itself every morning.

The same symbol can be seen in Greek culture as the Egyptians did pass it onto the Phoenicians who brought it to Greece. The name "Ourobos" was actually given to it by the Greeks.

We are more familiar with the symbol as a representation of infinity.

- **Amenta**

In Egyptian culture, this symbol represents the Underworld, or the land of the dead. Originally, however, it was used to symbolize the horizon where the sun set. After some time, it became a representation of the Nile's west bank—the place where the Egyptians would bury their deceased. This is the reason why the Amenta eventually became associated with the Underworld.

- **Scarab Beetle**

Scarabs are among the most important symbols in Ancient Egyptian culture. Also known as the dung beetle, they represented the sun, transformation, and the recreation/resurrection of life. Note that according to some scholars, the Egyptians confused the eggs laid and buried in the sand by the female beetles with the dung they rolled as the beetle's food source. In turn, the ancient Egyptians were potentially under the belief that the scarab was able to create life out of nothing.

- **The Feather of Maat**

You've read many mentions of this feather throughout this book so far and there's a good reason behind that. The Feather of Maat is one of the most commonly used symbols in hieroglyphics. This feather is believed to have been weighed against a deceased heart upon entering the Hall of Two Truths. As the myth goes, if a souls heart has been found to be equal or lighter to the feather's weight, it means that they have been virtuous in life and would be granted entry to Aaru. Aaru is the paradise presided over by Osiris. However, should the heart be heavier than the feather, it doomed that individual had not lived a respectable life and their heart would subsequently be devoured by Ammit. In effect, the soul would be cursed to remain in the Underworld for eternity.

CHAPTER THREE

Funerary Rituals in Ancient Egypt

For the Ancient Egyptians, the afterlife referred to "The Field of Reeds" which was a mirror-image of the life they lived on earth. These burial and funerary rituals have been in practice even as early as 4000 BCE and encapsulates their vision of what eternity is. These rites may have changed over time, but the focus remained the same— the certainty of existence beyond death. In fact, this belief in the afterlife became widespread throughout the ancient world through trade. It has influenced many other religions and civilizations, some scholars also believe that it served as the inspiration behind Christianity's own vision of eternal life, and has also become a major influence for other burial practices seen in different cultures around the world.

As Herodotus wrote:

> *As regards mourning and funerals, when a distinguished man dies, all the women of the household plaster their heads and faces with mud, then, leaving the body indoors, perambulate the town with the dead man's relatives, their dresses fastened with a girdle, and beat their bared breasts. The men too, for their*

> *part, follow the same procedure, wearing a girdle and beating themselves like the women. The ceremony over, they take the body to be mummified.* (Nardo, 110)

Mummification was being used as part of their funerary rites from as early as 3500 BCE. It is thought that the process was inspired by the way corpses were preserved when buried in the hot desert sand. The preservation aspect was important for the Ancient Egyptians as per their concept of the soul, one needed to have an intact body left on earth for them to experience an eternal after life. The ancients believed that the soul was comprised of nine different parts:

- Khat - the physical body
- Ka – our double form
- Ba – the human-headed bird aspect which was capable of speeding between earth and the heavens
- Shuyet – the shadow self
- Akh – the transcended, immortal self
- Sahu and Sechem – both aspects of the Akh
- Ab – the heart and also the source of good and evil
- Ren – our secret name

To exist, the Khat needed both Ka and Ba so that it would be able to recognize itself, thus the need for the body's preservation. After a person dies, their family would take their body to the embalmers (yes, even back then, this was an official occupation) where the professionals working there would produce specimens made out of wood, which are then graded in terms of quality. There were three different levels of quality and these vary in terms of price; the decision is left up to the deceased's family. The most expensive option, and also the best, is said to be representative of Osiris. These options also dictated the type of coffin the body would be buried in, the funerary rites involved, as well as the treatment of the body.

The Process of Mummification: Three Types

In the most expensive options, much care is put into working on the body. It was laid out on the table and the brain is removed. As graphic as this might be, this is done through the nostrils using an iron hook. What the hook cannot reach would then be flushed out using drugs. Next, the cavity would then be properly cleaned and not with ordinary water. It is cleaned using palm wine and yet another clean with a mixture of ground spices. Once the body is considered clean, the cavity is then filled with cassia, pure myrrh, and a number of other aromatic substances with the exception of frankincense. The cavity is then sewn up again after then the body is moved to natron and covered from head to toe for exactly seventy days.

After the seventy day period is done, the body would then be washed and the wrapping begins. They used linen strips and smeared the underside of it with gum before applying it to the body. In this condition, the body is sent back to the family who already have a wooden case made where the mummified corpse would be placed in.

The second most expensive option differed in the sense that less care was afforded to the deceased body. No incision was made to the body and the intestines were not taken out. However, oil of cedar is injected into the body through the use of a syringe-like tool. This is done through the anus which is later blocked up in order to keep the oil from escaping. Similar to the most expensive option, the body is also left to cure in natron for seventy days. After this period, the oil is drained out. Now, the effect of the oil can be so powerful that it actually dissolves viscera—along with the flesh which leaves the body as nothing more than skin and bones. Once the treatment is over, the body is then returned to the family.

The cheapest method of embalming was simply performed to flush out the intestines and cure the body in natron for seventy days. The internal organs were, of course, removed to make sure the corpse is preserved properly but because they believed these parts will be needed later, they are kept in canopy jars and sealed within the tomb. Only the heart is left inside the body.

Even the poorest members of society were given some form of ceremony, following their belief that if the deceased was not properly buried their spirits would return as ghosts and cause trouble to the living. Now, as the mummification process can be very expensive—even the cheapest option—the poor offered their own used clothing to the embalmers to use for wrapping the corpse. This act gave rise to "The Linen of Yesterday" which alludes to death. Eventually, this phrase became associated with anyone who had died, and was additionally used by the Kites of Nephthys who were the professional female mourners during funerals.

These women addressed the deceased as "one who was once dressed in fine linen, but now slept in the linen of yesterday". It must also be noted that the bandages used for wrapping the bodies were referred to as The Tresses of Nephthys after the goddess became associated with death and the afterlife. Unlike the richer members of society, the poor were buried in much simpler graves together with the artifacts they were fond of in life.

Artifacts and Provisions

Every grave contained some type of provision meant for the deceased to take with them into the afterlife. This includes the tombs as well—which were originally no more than simple graves dug into the earth but eventually formed into the rectangular mastabas we're familiar with today. This is done with the use of mud bricks. The pyramids would come into trend at a later period. First came the step pyramids then the "true pyramids" which many of us are most familiar with.

Tombs were inherently important in this culture, but their importance further increased as the Egyptian civilization progressed. These tombs were meant to protect the final resting place of the deceased's body, the Khat, from the elements as well as the widespread attacks from grave robbers. The sarcophagus were also built sturdier. Not only did they serve a symbolic purpose, they were also designed to protect and prevent any form of damage to the corpse.

*Note that the line of hieroglyphics which run down the back of a sarcophagus is meant to represent the deceased individual's backbone. It is also thought to provide strength for the mummy when rising to eat and drink.

As for the provisions, what is left in the tombs and graves vary depending on the person's wealth. That said, there were a number of common artifacts and among which include the Shabti Dolls. But, what are they for? To provide some background, the Egyptians were a society who were often called upon to volunteer a certain amount of time each year to building different projects. If they were ill or were not able to fulfill this duty for some other reason, they can send a replacement worker. Now, with that in mind, the Shabti Dolls are representations of these replacement workers. They are there to take the deceased persons place should they be called upon Osiris for service.

These dolls are also markers of wealth. The more dolls there are in a tomb, the wealthier the person is. This is because much like on earth, the replacement workers can only be used once, thus the need to create more dolls. In fact, the demand was so great that it fostered an entire industry dedicated to creating them.

Funeral Rites

After the mummification process and once the tomb had been prepared, the funeral would then be held. Much like modern funerals, the deceased is honored and mourned. There was also a funeral procession and during the burial, the Kites of Nephthys were there to lament loudly—this is a job they were paid for. They also sang songs such as The Lamentation of Isis and Nephthys. The ancients also believed that remembrance of the dead helped ensure their existence in the afterlife. In fact, all the outpouring of grief that happens at a funeral is also echoed in the Hall of Truth (also known as the Hall of Osiris) where the departing soul was heading to.

Chapter Four

Slavery in Ancient Egypt

When it comes to slavery in ancient Egypt, the controversy remains. This stems from the differences in opinion on how slavery is actually defined. For example, the term HEM (hm) translates to "slave" and was used to refer to someone who has less rights and was dedicated to a particular service. Then there were also the foreign slaves who were mainly from Asia. They were either traded by slave merchants or were prisoners of war. However, their period of enslavement in Egypt was limited. These prisoners of war or debt slaves were actually set free after serving for a certain period of time.

There were also slaves who served as personal attendants of different individuals. They often belonged to noblemen and estates of temples; these people were often captured during military campaigns or were bestowed as gifts by the king. However, what most scholars can agree on is the uncertainties with regards to this type of servitude; whether it was voluntary and comparable to what is typically imposed to a debtor who is unable to pay off his dues is still unknown.

Types of Enslavement in Ancient Egypt

1. Debt

Some Egyptians were, in fact, sold into slavery as a means to pay off their debt whilst there are those who sold themselves into slavery as a means of escaping poverty. Note that an indentured slave does keep some of their civil rights and in some cases, the economic security brought on by this new status is worth giving up their freedom for. Debt slavery was abolished during the Late Dynastic Period.

2. Punishment

In Ancient Egypt, the vizier was given the authority to impose perpetual forced labor on a person who has been convicted guilty of a crime—basically placing the person in a position of slavery for the rest of their days.

3. Voluntary Servitude

There have been pieces of information which suggest that women can pay temples to become a servant in it. However, as previously mentioned, there is much uncertainty on whether this is similar to the kind of bondage imposed on people who become slaves out of debt or selling themselves into the trade.

4. War

There have always been "slaves" in Egypt since the start of its history, however, the numbers increased significantly during the New Kingdom. This was when the pharaohs began committing to policies which involved participating in conquests to foreign countries—including Canaan, Syria, and Nubia. As a result, this brought many prisoners of war into the kingdom. The people who were enslaved in this manner included those of all status; some were tribe chiefs, captains, and so on.

During the campaigns of Thutmose III, the prisoners of war were taken and enslaved as a tribute given by the defeated. To provide you with statistics and a visual of just how significant these campaigns were, in one particular record, it was said that there were 691 prisoners of war taken, including 48 mares. In another, there were 295 male and female slaves and 68 horses taken.

It was also during Thutmose's reign that he received eight male and female black slaves from the Hittites which were tributes to him. This is valuable information as the Hittites must have seen these people as "presents" and of significant value for black people was a rarity amongst them. Nations, such as Nubia, who were defeated by the Egyptians during conquest also paid taxes to the crown—this also included slaves as a means of payment.

The least fortunate of the enslaved were sent to work in the copper and gold mines of both Nubia and Sinai. The conditions in these places were dreadful and according to the Greeks, water was merely rationed to the slaves and thus many died from dehydration mixed with exhaustion from the desert heat. It must also be noted that not all the prisoners of war were enslaved, some of them were inducted into the army.

The slaves placed into service for the royal family are considered to be the luckiest ones. In fact, their lives were a slightly more bearable than that of the peasants. The offspring of slaves, whether they be foreign or Egyptian, that showed exceptional skill or talent, became indispensable to the masters they served and even rose to high positions within the bureaucracy. In some cases, they may have even married into their former master's family after they've been set free.

The Treatment of Slaves

Despite the fact that slaves were at the bottom when it came to Egyptian society, they weren't treated as bad as other slaves in other societies. Servants at temples or those who served in the household of richer families lived a life that was comparably better than that of "free peasants".

It should also be noted that treating one's slave well is considered to be a moral precept, however the mere fact that this needs to be a moral duty points to the fact that slaves must have experienced unjust treatment quite often. In the Book of the Dead, included among a person's virtues for them to be able to join the company of the gods in the afterlife included:

I have not domineered over slaves.

I have not vilified a slave to his master.

Chapter Five

Ancient Egyptian Warfare and Famous Battles

Ancient Egypt was one of the very first civilizations, it is also among the first who adopted a hierarchical society. A really interesting fact about Egypt is that no wars occurred until halfway through their existence. Scholars suggest that one reason behind this is the geographical boundaries that the kingdom had, such as the river Nile, which was difficult for attackers to cross.

That said, this does not mean that these borders kept the ancient Egyptians from raiding nearby countries. They had many conquests, looting various countries of precious metals, animals, and even people who eventually were condemned to slavery. These were not full blown wars, however.

Ancient Egyptian Weaponry

The ancients were known to have used siege warfare weapons, which included siege towers and battering rams. They commonly used a mix of melee and ranged weapons. These included clubs and maces, bows and arrows, spears, knives, javelins, axes, swords, and daggers. They also wore very little body armor and carried a rather simple shield to protect themselves. The soldiers also made use of chariots during battles.

Hyksos Invasion

It was around the year 1650 BC that the Hyksos people of the Northern Nile Delta made an attempt to invade Egypt. They managed to take control of the Northern Egyptian lands with very little resistance and confrontation. This invasion led to the Hyksos having control over the lands for an entire century. There are people who argue that this was a drawback for the great kingdom, but many believe that this event was the catalyst for improvements in Egypt's military stature. They did, eventually, wage war against the Hyksos Empire.

Under Seqenenre Tao (II) and Apophis, the Ancient Egyptians waged war against the Hyksos and were to force them out of Northern Egypt forever.

Egypt and the Canaanite

Before the battle against the Hyksos, warfare had already began in Ancient Egypt starting at around 1500 BC. This was not because of any invaders, however, and merely occurred because of the Egyptians want to further expand their lands, as well as their political control over the region. The first well-known war that Egypt participated in was against the Canaanite coalition. This occurred along the coastal region of Lebanon, Israel, Syria, and eventually moved into Turkey.

During this war there was one renowned battle referred to as *"The Battle of Megiddo"*, where Pharaoh Thutmose III sent 10,000 to 20,000 of his men to face off with an army of 10,000 to 15,000 which was led by the King of Megiddo and the King of Kadesh. This battle occurred in 1457 BC.

The Egyptians were able to surprise the Canaanite forces by camping close to where their outpost, effectively overwhelming their foes and sending them into full retreat. During this battle, the Egyptians were able to kill 83 Canaanite soldiers and captured around 400 prisoners. This outcome also meant that the Egyptians would have to lay siege to the city, which they did for a total of seven months before the city finally surrendered. The Egyptians won the war and expanded their lands across the region, furthering its borders.

Egypt and the Hittites

Another of the more well-known Egyptian wars was waged against the Hittites, during the Battle of Kadesh in 1288 BC. Under Rameses II, the Egyptians faced off against the Hittites who were led by Muwatalli II. This occurred at the plains just outside the city of Kadesh or as we know of the country today, Syria.

According to known history, the Egyptians came with 20,000 men and only 10,000 of which were engaged in the actual battle. The Hittites, on the other hand, had a massive cavalry of over 50,000 men. This battle also marked the biggest chariot battle in history, with over 6,000 chariots between the armies involved.

In terms of location, the actual place of battle came as a surprise to the Egyptians as they were told by Nomad travelers that the Hittites were camped 200 kilometers north of the Egyptians current location. This put the Egyptians at a disadvantage as Rameses believed that he would be able to take the city without opposition, thus rushing to it, but in the process he scattered his four divisions in different places.

The Hittites moved first, sending a massive chariot attack on the "Ri", one of the Egyptian divisions, and effectively annihilating it. They then moved to attack the "Anum", a second Egyptian division, which was also decimated, though there were a few who were able to escape the massacre. This second success made the Hittites believe that they had won, thus they began to loot whatever they could from the dead soldiers—however, this would prove to be their biggest mistake.

The remaining Egyptian divisions combined and proceeded to make a counterattack, routing the Hittite chariot force and killing nearly all of the Hittites aside from the few who managed to escape by swimming across the river, back to the rest of the Hittite army. The final battle happened the day after, when the Hittites launched another attack; this resulted in an absolute bloodbath, and both sides lost many soldiers.

In the end, the Hittites had to retreat across the river to where they were camped the previous day. Both sides claimed victory during this battle, though as history shows, it ended in a stalemate. The Egyptians were not able to further their land, whilst the Hittites were not able to continue on battling due to both dwindling resources and logistical complications.

CHAPTER SIX

Volcanic Eruptions and Revolts in Ancient Egypt

Whilst Ancient Egypt has a long list of great rulers, they were not spared from instances of revolt from its people. This can be easily attributed to inept leadership, but a new study suggests that there may be other things at play too. In this case, volcanic eruptions that happened half a world away may have also impacted the country's climate, leading to a series of unfortunate events that would eventually culminate in social unrest.

From its very beginnings, ancient Egyptian society relied heavily on summer monsoon rains which caused the river Nile to flood. This annual event allowed for agriculture to thrive along its fertile banks. It is this period that various historians are looking into—specifically, the ice-core data of various eruption dates which were collected in Antartica and Greenland. According to an authority on the Ptolemaic Dynasty, these eruptions—oddly enough—also coincided with some of the biggest uprisings in Egypt. This usually happened within one or two years after the eruptions.

This led researchers to believe that the volcanic eruptions may have caused a change in weather patterns, suppressing the annual monsoon rains which the Egyptians relied on, thus leading to poor harvests and drought. Of course, with the lack of resources, civil unrest was quite inevitable. It must also be noted that volcanoes were quite active during the Ptolemaic era—a rather unfortunate natural event as massive eruptions were occurring at a rate of two to three every 10 years.

So what causes the weather changes? As volcanoes erupt, they would release sulfurous gases into the stratosphere. These gases would then react and form aerosol particles, reflecting solar radiation into space which then leads to a cooling effect on earth. Without the sun's extra heat triggering the process of evaporation, the amount of rainfall is greatly reduced— in this case, it also stopped the monsoon winds which pushed rainwater into the headwaters of the river Nile.

While it is likely that the rulers were able to store away grain, the effects of volcanic eruptions could also last for several years—and for a growing kingdom, stored grain can only last for so long. Within two years of a huge volcanic eruption, historians have noted that eight out of the ten biggest revolts during the Ptolemaic era occurred. The largest of which was the Theban Revolt.

This lasted for twenty years, beginning in 207 BC, just two years after a volcanic eruption. During the reign of Cleopatra VII, within the final years of the Ptolemaic reign, two massive eruptions occurred in 46 BC and 44 BC which led to a string of agriculture failures. By the end of Cleopatra VII's reign, the land was suffering from a variety of social issues, including: plague, famine, inflation, rural depopulation, administrative corruption, as well as migration and land abandonment.

The Roman conquerors were quite fortunate in that the two centuries which followed saw a decrease in major volcanic eruptions.

CHAPTER SEVEN

The Seven Year Famine

This is an Ancient Egyptian narrative which was discovered by Charles Wilbour upon a rock on the Island of Sahal back in 1890.

It begins that in the eighteenth year of King Tcheser's reign, the whole southern region, the district of Nubia, and the Island of Elephantine were all under the rule of the high official Mater. The king was gripped by immense pressure because the Nile had not gifted the land with its annual inundation, thus leaving it barren. Food was scarce and the people had begun to resort to robbing their neighbors. Everywhere in the kingdom, there were children who cried out for food. Men, even the younger ones, held no strength—with some even collapsing due to the lack of nutrition. The elderly suffered greatly, too, finding no will to continue, and laid themselves on the ground awaiting death.

During this terrible time, the king sought Imhotep, a god and the son of Ptah of the South Wall. He was said to have delivered Egypt from a similar crisis once, but has not provided aid to the kingdom since. In his absence, the King asked the Mater to tell him of the place where the Nile rose, and who among the deities had tutelary duty over it.

In response to the king's urgent request, the Mater swiftly made his way and provided all the information which had been asked from him. He told the king that the Nile flood began at the Island of Elephantine, where the first city was brought into existence, and from this city rose the Sun who then went forth and blessed man with life. The spot on the island where the river rise was called Qerti; a double cavern which resembled two breasts and from which all good thing flowed from.

This cavern was also referred to as "the couch of the Nile" and from this post, the Nile-god stood watch until the day of inundation drew close. On the day itself, he would rush forward mightily, filling the whole country. In Elephantine, this god rose to a height of twenty-eight cubits whilst in Diopolos Parva, in the Delta, he would only rise to seven. This god was Khnemu and he was considered guardian of the flood. Keeping the doors that held the waters and releasing them when the appropriate time comes.

Mater continued to tell the king of the temple dedicated to Khnemu situated in Elephantine and told his royal master about the other gods, such as Anqet, Sopdet, Nephthys, Shu, Hapi, Nut, Geb, Isis, Horus, and Osiris. He also told him of the different items found in the area and that from these items, offerings must be made to Khnemu. Upon hearing this valuable information, the king offered tributes to the god, and eventually made his way to the very temple he was told of, in order to personally worship the Nile-god.

Eventually, Khnemu would appear before the king and to him he said, *"I am Khnemu the Creator. My hands rest upon thee to protect thy person, and to make sound thy body. I gave thee thine heart... I am he who created himself. I am the primeval watery abyss, and I am the Nile who riseth at his will to give health for me to those who toil. I am the guide and director of all men, the*

Almighty, the father of the gods, Shu, the mighty possessor of the earth."

The god promised that the Nile would overflow every year, just as it did during the olden times, and spoke of the good which would come upon the land once he has ended the famine. After the god had spoken, the king recalled of the deity's complaints about his shrine—that no one was looking after it, thus it had fallen into disrepair, despite the fact that the materials to accomplish the task was plentiful on the island itself.

As such, the king swiftly decreed that certain areas on either side of the Nile near Elephantine would be bordered and given to the temple of Khnemu. Tax was also imposed on every product produced by the neighborhood which was to be used for maintaining the god's priesthood. As the original text for this decree was written upon wood, it would not last the ages, thus the king ordered that a copy be put to stone and set in a place of prominence.

Though nothing is said about whether or not Khnemu kept his promise, we can safely assume that he did.

CHAPTER EIGHT

Tales from Ancient Egypt

The Shipwrecked Sailor

In the period when Pharaoh Amen-em-het reigned over Egypt, he was able to bring peace and prosperity to a kingdom that had been besieged with civil war and revolt for almost two hundred years. During his rule, many traders and adventurers journeyed to the south on expeditions, going up the Nile through Nubia and even reaching lands as far as Ethiopia. They sailed through the Red Sea and into the Indian Ocean where they found the enigmatic land of Punt, bringing back with them an array of treasures—including spices and jewels.

In the Royal Court, ship captains and expedition leaders awaited their turn to speak to the pharaoh and tell him of their stories, each one vying to be commissioned for a royal venture. Our tale begins on a day no different from the others, a wanderer approached the Grand Vizier in the palace at Thebes and begged to be introduced to the Pharaoh. He talked of great riches and of a magic island in the sea, located far to the south, and beyond both Nubia and Ethiopia.

However, the Grand Vizier was accustomed to such pleas and looked upon the wanderer with much doubt. Even threatening the others, informing them that they would be thrown out of the palace should their tale be unsatisfactory and full of fantastical ideas like the ones before them. But the wanderer did not back down and proceeded to regale the Grand Vizier with his story. He began:

"I was journeying to the mines of the pharaoh aboard a great ship which was rowed by one hundred and fifty sailors. These were men who had seen plenty, who were brave—with hearts stronger than lions. Together, we rowed and sailed for countless days along the Red Sea and into the ocean that lay beyond it. The captain and his steersman both swore to their knowledge of the weather, that the wind would not grow stronger but be just enough to help us voyage further.

It wasn't long before ill weather began to brew and eventually forced us towards land. Monstrous waves broke over the ship and like powerful talons, crushed it against the rocks. I managed to hold onto a piece of wood before jumping into the raging sea just as the ship hit ground. Every man aboard it perished and I could only watch as another great wave rushed towards me, sending me onto the shore. I crawled as strongly as I could in order to get away from the raging waters and found myself in the shelter of trees.

When the storm passed and dawn came upon me, I could not thank the gods enough for delivering me where all others have perished. But I came to realize, soon after, that I was on an island with no companion and no resources—though that mattered little for this island was different from any other that I have seen before. Food was readily available and came in the form of grapes and figs, grain, berries, and herbs. There were also fishes and birds, all for the taking.

I sated my hunger with the fruits at first, but by the third day I kindled a fire and made my first offering to the goods. Then I cooked meat and fish for my own sustenance. It was after this meal when I first heard the terrifying noise, so great was my fear that I flung myself onto the ground, and waited with bated breath for what was to come. The trees lashed about and I felt strong winds, no different from the storm I had survived not long before—but no wave came. When I had gathered enough courage to do so, I looked up and around me.

I shall never forget what I saw moving towards me.

A massive serpent of about thirty cubits long, his body covered with gold scales which changed into blue around its eyes—an entrancing lapis lazuli. The serpent approached me, its entire length coiled up near where I lay, its gigantic head looming above me. When it spoke, the fear in me grew even more.

What has brought you into my island, little one? Tell me at once for if you refuse, I will show you what it is like to burn alive and turned into nothing. Speak swiftly, I await to hear what I have not heard before!

Then it seized me within its jaws and carried me into its cave. Despite having held me in his sharp teeth, I was unscathed. Once more, he repeated the same question and it took all of my courage and strength to provide it with an answer. I bowed before it, treating the creature with the same reverence as if I was speaking to the Pharaoh himself.

I sailed under the command of the Pharaoh, Amen-em-het, aboard a great ship to bring back treasures from the mines in the south. However, we were assailed by a tempest which dashed our ship upon the rocks of this island. Every one, except for myself, perished. I was cast into the island by a wave and have been surviving off of the land for three days.

The serpent hissed back to me:

Fear not, little one, nor show any sadness in your face. If you have come upon my island in this way when your companions have all perished, it must be the will of the gods. For they have placed you in the safety of this island where there is nothing lacking, where all is good. Now, I shall tell you of the future. Here you will stay as one month adds itself to another; in four months a ship from Egypt shall come and take you back to your home safety. You shall die in your own land be laid to rest in the tomb which you have prepared.

Now, I shall tell you of this island. A tale which you can pass onto your Pharaoh. I dwell here with my brethren and my children, seventy-five serpents in all. But there is one stranger among us, a beautiful maiden who appeared in this island in a peculiar way—but she has since turned into ashes, having befallen the fire of heaven. As for you, I do not believe that the same fate awaits. Should you dwell here with patience, you will eventually be able to make your way back home to your wife and children.

I bowed to him in thanks and told him that I will speak to the Pharaoh of his greatness. That I will bring tributes of perfumes, sacred oils, and incense—the likes of which are offered similarly to the gods in their temples. I vowed to the great serpent that I will speak of the wonders of his island and that the Pharaoh shall send out another ship filled with the treasures of Egypt as gifts to his majesty. But, my words were met with laughter, for the great serpent knew of the riches kept within his island. He also knew that I would not be able to fulfill any of the vows I had made, *"For when you have left this island, you will vanish and return to your life without ever seeing it again. I do not doubt that the gods will reveal it once more to some other wanderer, such as yourself."*

With this understanding, I dwelt in the island happily, and the four months of my stay felt too short. When the day of my leave grew near, the silhouette of a ship made itself apparent in the horizon. I swiftly climbed up a tree to see better and there was no doubt that they were men of Egypt. I made my way to the serpent king's home to inform him, but he already knew and bid me farewell. I bowed and thanked him, and before I left, provided me with gifts of perfumes.

I took with me, sweet woods and cassia, cypress and kohl. The serpent king also gifted me with other precious things such as ivory and incense. When I had made my way onto the ship, the island itself seemed to move away from us, floating light as a feather and carried aloft by the sea. Then, night fell suddenly and when the moon illuminated the calm waters, the island was nowhere to be seen. The ship continued north and by the second month, we finally arrived in Egypt.

I hastened my way here, crossing the desert to ask this of you. To allow me to meet with the Pharaoh so that I may inform him of my adventure and so that I may give to him the gifts bestowed by the King of Serpents. I will ask that he allow me to commander a royal ship, to sail back out into the sea in search of Punt."

When the wanderer's tale had come to a close, the Grand Vizier only laughed heartily, telling the wanderer that whether the story was real or not, he would grant him an audience with the pharaoh—for he knew the ruler would delight upon hearing it. And so it goes that Amen-em-het was so enthralled by the wanderer's tale that he ordered to have it written by his chief scribe, Ameni-amen-aa, upon a roll of papyrus so that it may be read by others for eras to come.

The Battle of Horus and Set

This battle between Horus and Set takes on many different forms, there are versions of it that are more detailed and complex—especially as the stories evolve over time. However, one thing remains identical in all of these versions, and that is what the two deities are quarreling over. Horus and Set are in a contest over the right of succession to the throne, over kingship on earth.

The story begins after Osiris' death, having been murdered by his own brother, Set, and his limbs scattered throughout the earth. He is later revived by Nephthys and Isis, who searched for the missing pieces of his body until they were able to put him back together. It was after this event that Horus was conceived by Isis and Osiris.

Horus was initially hidden away by his mother to protect him from Set. She successfully achieves this by keeping him in the papyrus marshes. Isis will serve as the young god's protector and advocate, while Horus was entirely dependent upon his mother, and the powerful magic which she possessed. When he came of age, he approached the assembly of gods to ask for his legitimate right to the throne. Horus aims to assume kingship and depose of Set as a usurper.

The council appears to support this claim, but Horus receives opposition from Re, who is the council head. Re believes that Horus is simply too inexperienced to rule the earth as king.

What followed then is a battle between Horus and Set. They engage in combat, with Osiris helping his son prepare before departing to his own kingdom in the underworld. The combat would involve endurance, magic, and skill. It will also test the deities' cleverness and wit as they look for ways to outsmart each other. There were also instances were both made use of strategies to tarnish the other's reputation among the assembly of gods.

The victory was awarded to Horus in the end, however, with Set suffering a number of losses and humiliations. The divine assembly eventually conceded into giving Horus authority over the earth as Set had proven himself incapable of performing the role. It did not end so badly for Set, however. Re offered him a consolation prize in the form of his two daughters, as well as a job.

Set was tasked to protect Re's barge every single day from Apophis, a chaos monster who resided in the sea of sky through which the barge must travel.

In some versions, Set was destroyed, though others show him as gaining a role in the order that is overseen by Horus. Here, Set is given a role that is well-suited to his talents as both trickster and mighty warrior. It is worth noting, however, that Horus is able to outwit Set despite these titles given to him.

This particular tale, though obscure in nature, does play an important role when it comes to the succession of Pharaohs in Ancient Egypt. At death, a pharaoh takes on the role of Osiris in the story and retains his royal identity even in the afterlife. He would, of course, leave behind an heir who would assume the vacated throne just as Horus did. In this manner, the continuity of their reign and the image of the divine pharaoh is maintained. Needless to say, it lends legitimacy to the belief that kingship in Ancient Egypt is of divine origins. A pharaoh is akin to a god and in death, this is only further elevated.

Conclusion

Throughout this book, we have revealed just how closely intertwined the lives of the people were with that of their gods. How their beliefs influenced their daily lives as well as how they proceeded with death.

We have been introduced to the different deities that comprise the Egyptian pantheon and learned about the roles they played, and how they helped shape the land and its people. These are deities and myths that have also influenced other societies beyond the border of ancient Egypt, going as far as Greece.

It is our hope that the contents of this book have helped you better understand what life was like for the ancient Egyptians. How mysterious their rites were and how these rituals played a significant role in society.

Lastly, may you take the stories contained herein and gain, not just knowledge, but also a bit of magic that the old kingdom was renowned for.